THE STORY OF
SERENA WILLIAMS

An Inspiring Biography for Young Readers

—— Written by ——
Shadae B. Mallory

—— Illustrations by ——
Tequitia Andrews

callisto
publishing
an imprint of Sourcebooks

To Cameron, whose unwavering
support and encouragement fueled
the writing of this book. Thank you
for always being there to lift me.

Library of Congress Cataloging-in-Publication Data

Names: Mallory, Shadae, author.
Title: The story of Serena Williams : an inspiring biography for young readers / written by Shadae B. Mallory.
Description: [Naperville, Illinois] : Callisto Publishing, [2024] | Includes bibliographical references.
Identifiers: LCCN 2023053248 (print) | LCCN 2023053249 (ebook) | ISBN 9798886509533 (hardcover) |
    ISBN 9798886509380 (trade paperback) | ISBN 9798886509595 (epub)
Subjects: LCSH: Williams, Serena, 1981—Juvenile literature. | Women
    tennis players–United States–Biography–Juvenile literature.
Classification: LCC GV994.W55 M36 2024 (print) | LCC GV994.W55 (ebook) |
    DDC 796.342092 [B]–dc23/eng/20231120
LC record available at https://lccn.loc.gov/2023053248
LC ebook record available at https://lccn.loc.gov/2023053249

This product conforms to all applicable CPSC and CPSIA standards.
Source of Production: Versa Press
Date of Production: April 2024
Run Number: 5038970

Printed and bound in the United States of America.
VP 10 9 8 7 6 5 4 3 2 1

CONTENTS

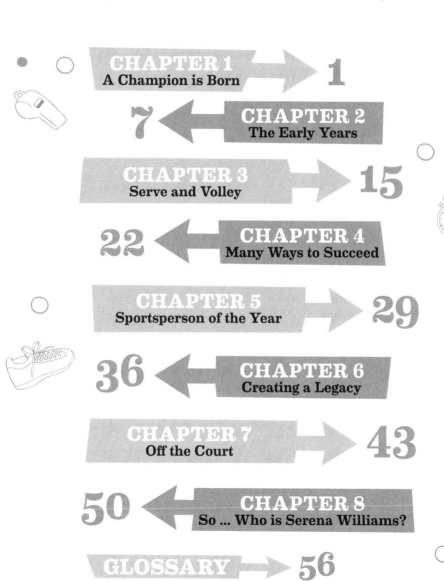

CHAPTER 1

A CHAMPION
IS BORN

◯ Meet Serena Williams ◯

When Serena Jameka Williams was a kid, she loved to play dress-up and do gymnastics. She spent a lot of time with her family, read books, and played games. Serena was an ordinary child. That changed when she picked up a tennis racquet. She became a **professional** athlete!

Serena started playing tennis when she was only three years old. With the help of her father and coaches, Serena and her older sister, Venus, worked hard to reach the top of their game.

Her sister and father helped Serena get better and better at tennis. Serena competed in her first **tournament** in 1995. She was only 14 years old. Serena did not win that first competition, but she did not let that stop her. Serena kept playing tennis and entering competitions. She has since won 23 **Grand Slam** titles.

JUMP
—IN THE—
THINK
TANK

Have you ever won an award for something you are good at? How did that make you feel?

66 There's one thing **I'm really** good at, and that's hitting the **ball over a net**, in a box. I'm **excellent.** **99**

Serena Williams is known as one of the best tennis players of all time. She won four gold medals at the **Olympic Games**. Serena changed the game of tennis forever.

◯ **Serena's World** ◯

Serena was born in Saginaw, Michigan, on September 26, 1981, to Oracene Price and Richard Williams. Serena has four older sisters: Yetunde, Lyndrea, Isha, and Venus.

At a young age, Serena and her family moved to Compton in Los Angeles County, California, where she began to play tennis.

Life in Compton was hard. Many Black people lived in Compton because of unfair local

laws and policies, and because other parts of Los Angeles County were too expensive. The Williams family made it work. Their family of seven lived in a two-bedroom house. Serena and Venus were **homeschooled** by their father. This gave them enough time for playing tennis *and* doing schoolwork. The Williams family lived in California until 1991. Then they decided to move to Palm Beach Gardens, Florida, so Venus and Serena could train with a talented tennis coach named Rick Macci.

Tennis is a very hard sport to play well. Having a good coach is important. To be good at tennis you have to be **flexible** and able to move your body into difficult positions. You have to be able to move *fast* and be strong. Some tennis players hit balls between 120 and 130 miles per hour! Serena had to learn to be fast and strong, and to have good balance, to become an amazing tennis player.

Serena would also need strength to handle the **racism** she would face as a Black athlete competing in a sport where most people were white. Sometimes people treated her differently because of the color of her skin. Her success and bravery inspired many Black children to play sports.

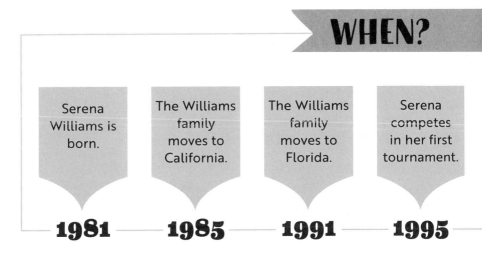

WHEN?

Serena Williams is born.	The Williams family moves to California.	The Williams family moves to Florida.	Serena competes in her first tournament.
1981	**1985**	**1991**	**1995**

CHAPTER 2

THE EARLY YEARS

An Athlete from the Start

Serena's father, Richard Williams, always knew Serena and Venus would be professional tennis players. In fact, he was so sure of his daughters' success that he wrote out a plan with everything Serena and Venus would need to become tennis champions. Richard kept his plan in a book along with information about all the best professional tennis players and coaches.

When Serena's older sister Venus started playing tennis, Serena wanted to play, too. Venus was only one year older than Serena and started playing tennis at four years old. Serena went to the tennis courts with her father and Venus almost every day. They practiced with their father at Compton Park. The Williams family liked to joke around by calling the park the "Compton Country Club." Usually, country clubs are fancy, but these courts were cracked and faded.

Serena and Venus were very competitive. The girls played against each other often when they practiced. Venus started competing in junior tennis tournaments in 1989. Serena wanted to enter, too, but her dad would not let her.

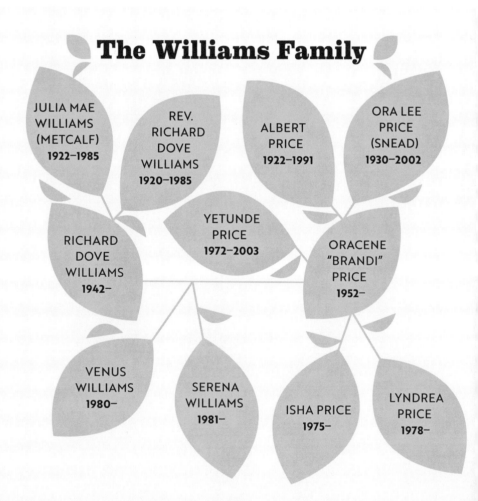

The Williams Family

JULIA MAE WILLIAMS (METCALF) 1922–1985

REV. RICHARD DOVE WILLIAMS 1920–1985

ALBERT PRICE 1922–1991

ORA LEE PRICE (SNEAD) 1930–2002

YETUNDE PRICE 1972–2003

RICHARD DOVE WILLIAMS 1942–

ORACENE "BRANDI" PRICE 1952–

VENUS WILLIAMS 1980–

SERENA WILLIAMS 1981–

ISHA PRICE 1975–

LYNDREA PRICE 1978–

Serena was determined to show off her skills. She entered a tournament by herself! While Venus competed in her game, Serena snuck away to compete in hers. Serena won her match and showed her dad she could compete just like Venus. Both girls did so well they ended up playing each other in the tournament finals. Venus won the match, but she gave Serena her first-place trophy.

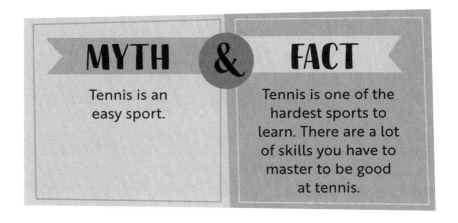

MYTH & FACT

Tennis is an easy sport.

Tennis is one of the hardest sports to learn. There are a lot of skills you have to master to be good at tennis.

A Rising Talent

When he saw his daughters in the junior tournaments, Richard realized how good they were. He knew they needed more training.

He decided to find them a better coach. In 1991, Richard called coaches all over the United States. Rick Macci, a talented tennis coach in Florida, was interested. He flew to California to meet Venus and Serena. Rick was impressed by how well the girls moved on the court. Venus and Serena had powerful swings, fast movement, and a lot of

WHERE?

CANADA

QUEBEC CITY

QUEBEC

CALIFORNIA

COMPTON

FLORIDA

PALM BEACH GARDENS

motivation. Rick wanted to help teach the girls tennis. The Williams family moved to Florida.

After leaving California, Serena and her sister stopped competing in junior tournaments. Richard wanted his daughters to focus on practicing and schoolwork. They practiced for three years without competing. Venus made her professional debut when she was 14 years old, in 1994. Serena followed in 1995, also at age 14. This meant they were in their first matches in a

JUMP
-IN THE-
THINK TANK

Have you ever failed at something you did your best at? How did you motivate yourself to try again?

professional league. It was called the Women's Tennis Association (WTA). These games counted toward their **ranking**.

Serena's first professional match was the Bell Challenge in Quebec City, Canada. She lost to Annie Miller, another American player. Serena felt sad and defeated after losing to Annie.

Although Serena did not win her first professional match, she kept practicing and practicing. She did not give up. Serena wanted to win the next time. She competed again the next year.

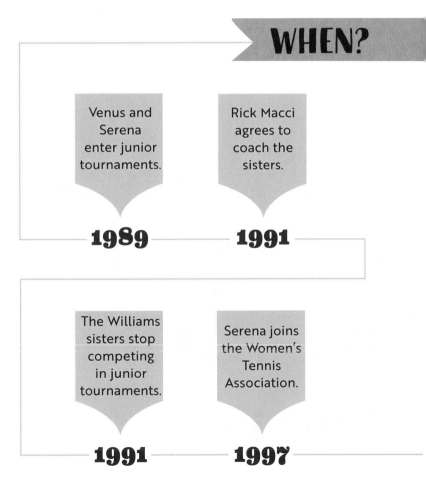

WHEN?

Venus and Serena enter junior tournaments.

Rick Macci agrees to coach the sisters.

1989 — **1991**

The Williams sisters stop competing in junior tournaments.

Serena joins the Women's Tennis Association.

1991 — **1997**

CHAPTER 3

SERVE AND VOLLEY

Tennis Twosome

Serena was eager to keep up with Venus. She continued to practice her serve and volley. A serve is the shot that starts the game. A volley is a shot where the ball is hit over the net before it ever touches the ground. Together, a serve-and-volley can be a powerful method to score a point. When done correctly, a volley is hard to hit back. Serena practiced many playing styles to make herself a competitive **opponent**—even for Venus! Because they played similarly, Serena had to find ways to be quick in order to defeat Venus.

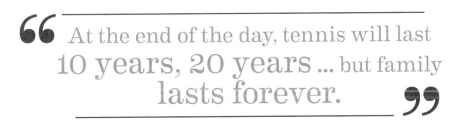

66 At the end of the day, tennis will last 10 years, 20 years ... but family lasts forever. 99

Serena faced a lot of challenges no matter how hard she trained or how much she practiced.

JUMP
–IN THE–
THINK
TANK

Do you have a
favorite outfit?
What does
it look like?
How do you
feel when you
wear it?

Tennis was usually played by white athletes, so Venus and Serena stood out. They were often seen differently because of the color of their skin, the powerful way they played, and their unique style. The Williams sisters loved to wear brightly colored clothes. They also liked to wear their hair in beaded braids. Many reporters and tennis fans made hurtful comments about their hair. They also said their clothes were distracting. The girls did not let others change who they were. They continued to wear braids, beads, and their favorite outfits as they competed in tournaments all over the world.

The sisters liked playing against each other, but they also played together. They made a great team in **doubles** matches. Together, they won many competitions.

16

◯ Little Sister Wins Big ◯

In 1998, Serena competed in the Australian Open. She won her first match and was so excited! Her next opponent was her sister Venus. It would be the first time Venus and Serena competed against each other professionally. Both girls played well, but Venus won. Losing only made Serena want to try harder. Serena loved the rivalry she had with Venus. It inspired her to keep training.

In tennis, there are four big tournaments, called **majors,** every year: the Australian Open, French Open, U.S. Open, and Wimbledon. Winning all four tournaments is called a Grand Slam.

In 1999, at age 17, Serena won the U.S. Open. Serena had finally beaten Venus at something— she won her first major tournament a whole year before her sister.

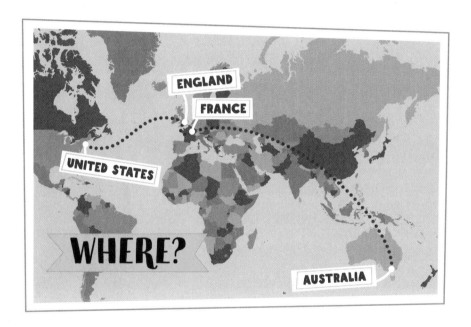

In 2000, Venus and Serena faced each other during the semifinals at Wimbledon. Venus won and made history as only the second Black woman to be a Wimbledon champion.

Later that year, Venus and Serena teamed up to play in the doubles competition at the 2000 Summer Olympics. Together they won their first gold medal. They went on to become the first sister team to ever win a major title in doubles, at the 2001 Australian Open.

Not every event went so well. Later in 2001, Venus and Serena played a tournament in Indian Wells, California. They were scheduled to compete against each other, but Venus got hurt. She could not play anymore. The match was called off only five minutes before it was supposed to start. Because it was short notice, some fans said Venus withdrew on purpose to allow

Serena to move on to the finals. That was not true. Venus really did have a bad injury.

The rest of the Indian Wells competition was horrible for Serena. When she arrived to play her next match, fans booed from the stands. They called her names and made her feel bad. Despite the crowd's attitude, Serena did her best and won the tournament. Serena was happy to have won, but because of the way she was treated, she never wanted to play at Indian Wells again.

WHEN?

Serena competes in the Australian Open.	Serena wins the U.S. Open.	The Williams sisters win gold in the Summer Olympics.	Serena competes in the Indian Wells tournament.
1998	**1999**	**2000**	**2001**

CHAPTER 4

MANY WAYS TO SUCCEED

◯ Setting Records ◯

As Venus and Serena started to play each other more often, Venus usually beat her younger sister and climbed in the rankings. When a player wins a match, they are given points by the Women's Tennis Association (WTA). These points are counted for every match within a 52-week period. Winning one or two big matches is not enough to be at the top of the rankings. Players must win many events to be number one. In February 2002, Venus was ranked number one in the WTA! Serena was determined to take her spot.

In 2002, Serena won her first French Open—defeating Venus in the final match. Within months, Serena sat at number two in the rankings, just behind Venus. Serena was not done yet. The same year, she beat Venus at both Wimbledon and the U.S. Open. Serena beat her sister a fourth time in the 2003 Australian Open. These four wins did not happen within the same year, so they were not considered a Grand Slam. But her **consecutive** wins were so impressive they got their own name: the "Serena Slam."

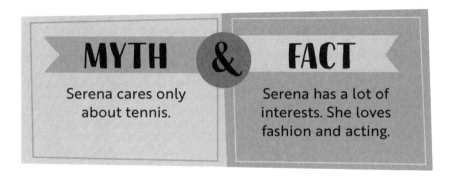

MYTH & FACT

Serena cares only about tennis.

Serena has a lot of interests. She loves fashion and acting.

Venus and Serena began following other dreams, too. Venus started an interior design company, V Starr Interiors. Serena started a fashion line, Aneres (that's Serena spelled backwards) by Serena Williams. Serena also loves acting. In 2001, she voiced a cartoon version of herself on the television show *The Simpsons*. By 2020, Serena had been in 26 movies and television shows.

JUMP
-IN THE-
THINK
TANK

Is there someone in your life you miss? What do you do to remember them or feel close to them?

⟨ New Challenges ⟩

In 2003, Serena and Venus experienced something more difficult than either of them could have imagined. On September 14, 2003, their oldest sister, Yetunde Price, died suddenly. Yetunde had stayed in Compton after the

Williams family moved to Florida. While her younger sisters became tennis superstars, Yetunde started a family in California.

The Williams family was shocked by Yetunde's sudden death. Everyone flew back to California to attend her funeral. Serena missed her big sister so much.

Losing her sister made the next few years very hard for Serena. On top of the heartbreak she felt for Yetunde, Serena also needed knee surgery. Serena's injuries prevented her from competing as often as she wanted. That made her even sadder. Her sadness made it hard to focus on tennis. She became **depressed** and needed to see a doctor for help. Sometimes when people are having a really hard time, doctors can help them get things back on track.

Serena slowly started to feel a bit better and was ready to play more matches. Before going to the 2007 Australian Open, she decided to travel to Ghana and Senegal in Africa. She wanted to help others in need by bringing food and medicine to different villages. Serena also gave tennis lessons and helped build a school in Senegal. Giving back to others helped Serena heal and grow. She got the strength she needed to win the 2007 Australian Open.

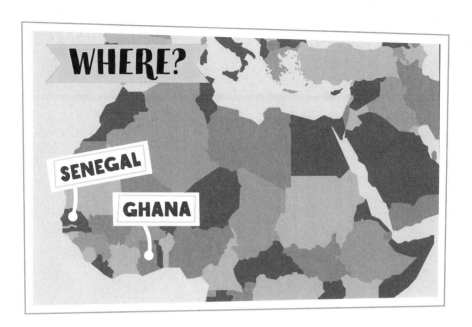

WHERE?

SENEGAL

GHANA

WHEN?

Venus is number one in the WTA rankings.	Serena takes number one in the WTA rankings.	Yetunde dies suddenly.	Serena wins the Australian Open.
2002	**2002**	**2003**	**2007**

CHAPTER 5

SPORTSPERSON OF THE YEAR

⚬ Highs and Lows ⚬

Getting back on track took time and effort
for both Venus and Serena. Soon they started
competing more frequently again. They were
even invited back to the Summer Olympics,
this time in Beijing, China, in 2008. Venus and
Serena won the gold medal for doubles again.
Their win reminded the entire world that Venus
and Serena were amazing players.

In 2009, Serena competed in the U.S. Open again. During one of her matches, Serena got upset with the **officials** at her game. She disagreed with one of the calls they made against her play. Out of frustration, Serena broke a rule and yelled at the officials. This caused her opponent to get a free point, and Serena ended up losing the match. She was also given a big fine: $82,500.

Serena did her best to move past the events of the U.S. Open and focus on what came next. But then in 2010, she stepped on broken glass while she was at a restaurant in Munich, Germany. The cut on her foot was so bad she had to get 12 stitches. Serena tried to keep a positive attitude. But she soon after her foot injury, got news that was really scary.

Serena learned she had blood clots in her lungs. This was a big problem that needed to get fixed right away. Blood clots are really dangerous!

She had surgeries to fix the clots right away. Because of her medical problems, many people thought Serena was going to **retire**. But Serena knew she would push through. With the support of her family, she regained her strength.

JUMP
—IN THE—
THINK
TANK

Think about a time you were scared. What gave you hope? Did someone help you stay strong?

◠ A Huge Honor ◠

By the time the 2012 Summer Olympics were being hosted in London, Serena was feeling much better. She had recovered from her surgeries and decided to play in the Olympic Games. She played alongside Venus in doubles, and she played singles, too. She won gold in both tournaments. This was the first time Serena won a gold medal for playing on her own at the Olympics.

Serena continued to recover from her setbacks. She played in the majors and continued to rank number one. In 2015, Serena even went back to Indian Wells, the tournament where she was booed in 2001. She was nervous, but excited and hopeful that things would be different this time. And things *were* different! Serena was amazed when she walked onto the court and heard people cheering for her. Everyone was happy to see Serena return.

> 66 Everyone always asked, 'What was your greatest moment in tennis?' I always said it hasn't happened. I think it has happened now... going back to Indian Wells and playing. 99

Serena's next few tournaments proved to everyone that she was stronger than ever. She won the final of the French Open right after being sick with the flu. Soon after, she won Wimbledon and secured her second Serena Slam.

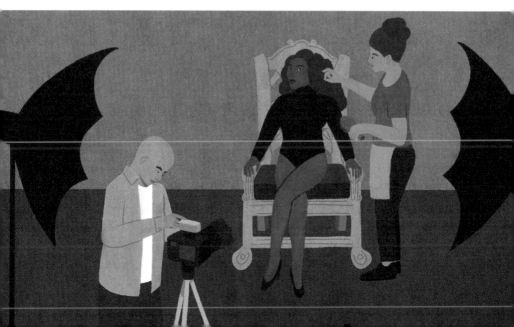

At the end of 2015, Serena was named Sportsperson of the Year by *Sports Illustrated*. She was the first Black woman to receive that huge honor. Serena kept making history and inspiring young girls all over the world.

WHEN?

Venus and Serena win gold at the Olympics.

Serena is fined $82,500 for yelling at an official.

Serena's injuries prevent her from playing.

2008 — **2009** — **2010–2012**

Serena wins her first solo gold medal.

Serena is Sportsperson of the Year.

2012 — **2015**

CHAPTER 6
CREATING A LEGACY

◯ The Greatest of All Time ◯

Serena continued to prove she was the best
of the best. She won her 700th match during
the 2015 Miami Open. Serena also held the top
ranking for two years in a row. She was named
the 2015 International Tennis Federation
Champion for the fourth year in a row.

Serena's 2015 season took her all over the
world. She competed in the Italian Open in May.
The morning of the tournament, Serena and her
friends were eating breakfast at their hotel.
A man named Alexis Ohanian sat at the table
next to them. Serena introduced herself and
invited Alexis to join their table. Serena and
Alexis enjoyed their meal together, and later
that day Alexis watched Serena's tennis match.

Serena and Alexis had fun together in Rome. Soon, Serena had to leave to play in the French Open. She invited Alexis to go to Paris with her, and to her surprise, he did! Alexis flew to Paris to watch Serena play. They spent a lot of time walking around the city, talking, and falling in love.

Serena and Alexis's love grew quickly. The two got to know each other very well. In December 2016, Alexis took Serena back to the hotel in Rome where they had met. He asked her to marry him. Serena was thrilled to say yes.

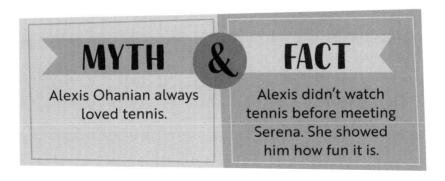

MYTH & FACT

Alexis Ohanian always loved tennis.

Alexis didn't watch tennis before meeting Serena. She showed him how fun it is.

◯ **Family Life** ◯

Less than a month later, Serena won the
2017 Australian Open. That was her 23rd major
tournament victory. With that win, she set
another record. At 35 years old, she was the oldest
woman to win a Grand Slam title. Serena holds
the most Grand Slam titles since professionals
and amateurs started competing together in 1967.
What is even more impressive is that Serena won
the tournament while she was pregnant.

Serena did not know she was pregnant when she competed in the Australian Open. Her body had not changed much. Serena did notice she felt a bit different. After the tournament finished, she decided to take a pregnancy test. It was positive! Serena and Alexis were very excited.

Their daughter, Alexis Olympia Ohanian, Jr., was born in September 2017 in West Palm Beach, Florida. Serena's time in the hospital was very scary. After giving birth, Serena began to lose feeling in her legs. She worried that it might be blood clots like the ones she had before. When Serena asked her doctors for help, they did not seem to be worried. Serena fought to have her doctors check for blood clots. When they finally agreed to run the tests, they discovered Serena was right. Serena had to have surgery to keep the blood clots from hurting her.

Thankfully, Serena knew her body and what she needed. Her experience in the hospital made her want to make sure nobody else had to work with doctors who did not believe them. This is a problem that is especially common for women of color. Serena felt that was unfair. She became an **activist**, helping women of color get better healthcare.

Soon after their daughter was born, Serena and Alexis got married in New Orleans.

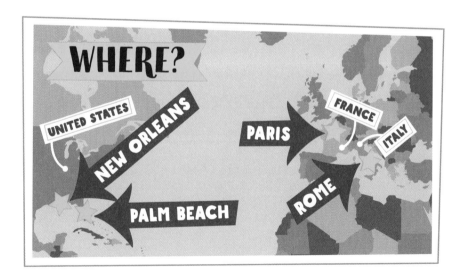

They were so happy with their new family!
Their second daughter, Adira River Ohanian,
was born in August 2023.

WHEN?

Serena wins her 700th match at the Miami Open.	Serena and Alexis meet in Rome.	Serena and Alexis get engaged.	Serena wins the Australian Open while pregnant.
2015	**2015**	**2016**	**2017**

CHAPTER 7
OFF THE COURT

◯ Great Works of Charity ◯

Serena has always cared about other people. She likes to help others when they need it. Serena has been doing charity work for a long time.

Serena **volunteers** with **UNICEF**. UNICEF is a charity that helps children all over the world get education and healthcare. In 2011, Serena was named a Global Ambassador by UNICEF. That meant she was a well-known person who supported the organization. As a Global Ambassador, Serena did a lot with UNICEF. In 2015, she was part of a UNICEF team that helped children in Ghana get important **vaccinations**.

After her work with UNICEF, Serena wanted to continue to help children in need. She created the Serena Williams Fund to help build schools in other countries. Over the years, the Serena Williams Fund has helped build schools in

Ghana, Jamaica, Uganda, Kenya, and Zimbabwe.

Serena also wanted to do something to honor her sister Yetunde. Serena worked with her family to create the Yetunde Price Resource Center (YPRC) in Compton. The YPRC has become a very important place in Compton. The center offers a safe space for

community members to learn about mental health, including how to get resources such as therapy. The YPRC also hosts the Harlem Junior Tennis and Education Program, which helps kids learn about tennis, processing their emotions, and living healthy lifestyles.

◯ Serena's Legacy ◯

Serena Williams has made a positive impact on the world around her. Her ability to rise to the top of the rankings proves that she is an amazing athlete. Serena had to overcome many challenges to be the best. Her success as a Black woman in a mostly white sport has made her a role model for children of color everywhere. The impact she has had on tennis is huge.

Serena's **advocacy** for others has made her a champion for change. She has **donated** her time and money to help important causes. Serena has made learning tennis possible for more kids from **underserved communities**.

Today, Serena Williams is still considered the best tennis player of all time. Her historic wins have earned her a place as one of the best athletes in the world. After her first daughter was born, Serena returned to tennis. She kept winning matches and even tournaments. At the

U.S. Open, she became the first player in history to reach the semifinals of a major tournament in four separate decades. Although in 2022, she announced her plans to retire, her place in history is guaranteed.

Serena continues to inspire people every day with her amazing story. She never let anyone stop her from following her dreams. Embrace your own dreams. Follow your heart, just like Serena does. Maybe you could break her record one day!

Make sure you're very courageous: be strong, be extremely kind, and above all be humble. 99

WHEN?

Serena is named a UNICEF Global Ambassador.	Serena works with UNICEF to build schools.
2011	**2015**

The Yetunde Price Resource Center opens.	Serena plays her 1,000th match.
2016	**2021**

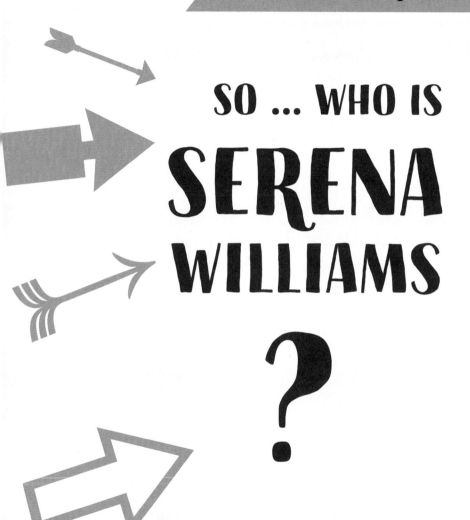

CHAPTER 8

SO ... WHO IS

SERENA WILLIAMS

?

◯ Challenge Accepted! ◯

Now that you know about Serena Williams's life and work, let's test your new knowledge in a little "who, what, when, where, why, and how" quiz. Feel free to look back in the text to find the answers if you need to, but try to remember the answers first.

1 **Where was Serena Williams born?**

→ A Philadelphia, Pennsylvania

→ B Tampa Bay, Florida

→ C Saginaw, Michigan

→ D Los Angeles, California

2 **How old was Serena when she started playing tennis?**

→ A Ten

→ B Five

→ C Seven

→ D Three

3 **Who coached Serena and Venus in Florida?**

→ A Rick Macci

→ B Richard Williams

→ C Annie Miller

→ D Patrick Mouratoglou

4 **What stood out about Serena's clothes during matches?**

→ A They were all black.

→ B They were brightly colored.

→ C They were designed by her mother.

→ D They always matched with Venus.

5 **When did Serena first compete in the Olympic Games?**

→ A 1996

→ B 2012

→ C 2000

→ D 2008

6 **Who or what did Serena name her fashion line after?**

→ A Her sister, Yetunde

→ B Her mother, Oracene

→ C Herself

→ D Her favorite food

7 **What injury stopped Serena from competing in 2012?**

→ A Her right hand

→ B Her foot

→ C Her back

→ D Her head

8 **Where did Serena meet her husband?**

→ A Sydney, Australia

→ B Washington, D.C.

→ C Rome, Italy

→ D London, England

9 **What tournament does Serena consider to be the high point of her career?**

→ A The U.S. Open

→ B The Bell Challenge

→ C Wimbledon

→ D Indian Hills

10 **How many Grand Slam titles has Serena won?**

→ A 23

→ B 18

→ C 29

→ D 15

◯ **Our World** ◯

Serena's influence on tennis is unmatched! Let's look at some of the other great things Serena has done.

→ When Serena was a little girl, the tennis courts she practiced on were cracked, faded, and unkept. Serena and Venus have helped provide better facilities for others. They helped remodel the Southeast Tennis Learning Center in Washington, D.C. Today, this facility helps hundreds of people learn tennis.

→ During the Covid-19 pandemic, Serena teamed up with companies to provide face masks to children. She wanted to make sure children could go back to school safely. Serena helped provide more than 4 million masks to school-aged children.

→ Serena also partnered with a company called Instacart during the Covid-19 pandemic. Together, they helped provide meals to people who needed food. Serena personally donated 50,000 meals!

→ As a woman in sports, Serena knows how hard it can be for girls to be seen as equal. In fact, girls are twice as likely to drop out of sports than boys. During the 2020 Olympic Games, Serena joined the "Just #WatchMe" campaign to show support for young women in sports.

JUMP
—IN THE—
THINK TANK FOR
≈ MORE! ≈

Serena's motivation to do her best helped her create a successful career. Perhaps her strength and courage have inspired you to do the same. Following are some more questions to inspire you to be number one at whatever you do!

→ Serena experienced many challenges in her career, but she never gave up! How do you think she motivated herself to keep going?

→ The Williams sisters have inspired millions of people with their story. What are some ways Serena's story can inspire you to do your best?

→ Serena likes to showcase her creativity through her fashion line, Aneres. How do you like to be creative? If you had a fashion company, what would you name it?

Glossary

activist: A person who works to bring about change for something they care very much about

advocacy: The act of defending or supporting a cause or person

consecutive: Following one another in order without gaps

depressed: Feeling sad and losing interest in activities you once enjoyed

donate: To give as a way to help a cause

doubles: In tennis, a match played between teams of two players

flexible: Able to bend easily

Grand Slam: The accomplishment of having won all four of the tennis majors in one year

homeschooled: Taught at home instead of in a school

majors: The four most important tennis tournaments (Australian Open, French Open, U.S. Open, and Wimbledon)

officials: The people who make sure the players and coaches follow the rules in sports games

Olympic Games: Athletic games held every four years, each time in a different country. Athletes from many nations compete.

opponent: A person you are competing against

professional: Skilled at a sport and paid to compete in it

racism: Discrimination against someone of a different race based on the belief that one's own race is better

ranking: A number given to a professional tennis player based on how well they've done in tournaments

retire: To stop working in a certain career

tournament: A series of contests played for a championship

underserved communities: Areas where people have limited access to resources like medical care

UNICEF: Stands for United Nations International Children's Emergency Fund, an organization that helps children in need

vaccinations: Treatments that help protect people from disease

volunteer: To spend time working for a cause without being paid

Bibliography

Daniels, Tim. "Serena Williams Returning for Wimbledon After Missing 2022 French Open." Bleacher Report, June 14, 2022. bleacherreport.com/articles/10038653-serena-williams-returning-for-wimbledon-after-missing-2022-french-open.

Jefferson, J'na. "Giving Back: Venus And Serena Williams To Launch 'Yetunde Price Resource Center' in Compton." Vibe, November 2, 2016. vibe.com/news/sports/venus-serena-williams-yetunde-price-resource-center-464341/.

Langmann, Brady. "Rick Macci Coached Venus and Serena Williams For Years. He Told Us What *King Richard* Left Out." *Esquire*, November 22, 2021. esquire.com/entertainment/movies/a38311899/rick-macci-king-richard-interview-true-story/.

Serena Williams. "Philanthropy." serenawilliams.com/pages/philanthropy

Williams, Serena. "Serena Williams: I'm Going Back to Indian Wells." *Time*, February 4, 2015. time.com/3694659/serena-williams-indian-wells/

About the Author

Shadae B. Mallory is a writer, educator, and social justice advocate. They primarily work in higher education, and are also a diversity, equity, and inclusion consultant. This is their second publication. You can follow them online at ShadaeMallory.com

About the Illustrator

Tequitia Andrews is an artist and illustrator from Richmond, Virginia. She enjoys illustrating strong, empowering women. Her illustrations have been used for book covers, greeting cards, puzzles, and picture books.

WHO WILL INSPIRE YOU NEXT?

EXPLORE A WORLD OF HEROES AND ROLE MODELS IN
THE STORY OF ...AN INSPIRING BIOGRAPHY SERIES
FOR YOUNG READERS.

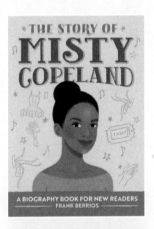

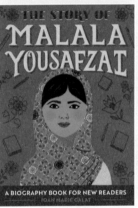

LOOK FOR THIS SERIES
WHEREVER BOOKS AND EBOOKS ARE SOLD